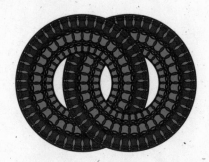

Impenitent Notes

Impenitent Notes

Baron Wormser

CavanKerry ◊ Press LTD.

CavanKerry Press Ltd.

Fort Lee, New Jersey

www.cavankerrypress.org

Library of Congress Cataloging-in-Publication Data

Wormser, Baron.
  Impenitent notes / Baron Wormser.
  p. cm.
  Poems.
  ISBN 978-1-933880-23-5 (alk. paper)
  I. Title.
  PS3573.O693I66 2011
  811'.54--dc22
  2010031552

Cover art Janet Wormser © 2010
Cover and interior design by Gregory Smith
First Edition 2010, Printed in the United States of America

NOTABLE VOICES
CavanKerry◦Press

CavanKerry Press is proud to publish the works
of established poets of merit and distinction.

CavanKerry Press is grateful for the support it
receives from the New Jersey State Council on the Arts.

Other Books by Baron Wormser

POETRY

The White Words (1983)

Good Trembling (1985)

Atoms, Soul Music and Other Poems (1989)

When (1997)

Mulroney and Others (2000)

Subject Matter (2004)

Carthage (2005)

Scattered Chapters: New and Selected Poems (2008)

PROSE

Teaching the Art of Poetry: The Moves (co-author, 1999)

A Surge of Language: Teaching Poetry Day by Day
(co-author, 2004)

The Road Washes Out in Spring:
A Poet's Memoir of Living Off the Grid (2006)

The Poetry Life: Ten Stories (2008)

Contents

III

IV

for Richard Miles

and to the memory of Jack Wiler

Impenitent Notes

I

Missile

In school you stuttered.

The brainy guys and the girls with lilac bows
    in silken hair mocked you,

The imbecile who never finished
    a sentence, who chased after words
    as if they were so many puppies,

Then stood before the class, face flushed,
    head lolling, tongue a humorous monster.

Even the young teacher who read a psalm
    daily and valued each wayward,
    misshapen life lost patience with you
    and smiled ruefully.

On the playground you tried to capture
    your tormentors but they eluded you,
    shouting threats at a safe distance
    while you seethed like a noose.

The death you brought was confused,
    dimly retributive, a shadow amid darkness.

Your grin out-grimaced gargoyles;
    your laugh pierced iron.

You wished to make time have a stop
    but your betters knew better—
    your hurt was an ever-available arrow.

Anguish sang in your empty eyes. Grief crowed.

Travel

The train swayed past cropped fields,
Barking collies, abandoned gas works, cows,
Brown bungalows with little gardens
And potting sheds, kids kicking a soccer ball
Down a deserted street. Behind me two teenage girls
Dressed in identical vests and white blouses talked.
"I hate people who are good," one of them said.
"They want you to be good too." "I know," the other one said.
"My Aunt Mary is like that. She makes me retch."
I rose and walked down the wobbling aisle toward
The space between cars. Two guys were sharing a pint
In the boyish, conspiratorial way men do.
I stretched my short legs and smiled at their whiskey.

Night creeping over the western hills, the lights of
The villages along ridges. I wanted to stride into
A house and be welcomed like a long-lost uncle.
I wanted to see everyone rise excitedly.
I wanted to smell the cooking, the wash, the closets,
The cats, the honest odors of bustling flesh.
I wanted to hug muslin, wool, linen.

The girls kept talking but in lower and tenser voices.
Two more stops to the terminus, a tiny station
From where I would take a ferry across a sea.
The coach windows beaded with the vapor
Of human warmth. I ran fingers along the jeweled moment
Before it died in the taunting arms of speech.

Buddy Holly

We're driving to town to buy groceries (brown rice,
Baking powder, raisins, safflower oil), flashlight
Batteries, sunflower seeds so the blue jays can continue
Lording it over the smaller birds that also want to eat,
And we start talking about how the U.S., which started
Out as the bravest promise the human spirit
Had made so far, the light of William Blake's
And many another's enraptured eye, became a homage
To vehicular motion: commoners having been freed
From the yokes that princes placed upon them
To transpire the vapors of octane desire.

"Invention overrules intention," my wife mutters
While fiddling with the car radio.
I begin to sputter my own homily
When suddenly Buddy Holly starts singing,
His voice twenty-one years old and staying there
As long as machines can play recordings.
"Ooh, ooh, ooh, Peggy Sue," he warbles
And so, simultaneously, do we, plus some finger popping
And rhythmic squirming within our seat-belted
    confinement.
He lights up another minute; then he's spent.

We keep tingling—savoring the pure thrall
Of foreshortened American joy.
He's the incalculable voice of poetry.
Our beautifully engineered beast rolls on.

Hebrew School (1955)

You sat at a long table in the cement
Floor cellar of the two-story wooden shul—
A shingled, ramshackle structure with weirdly
Narrow windows, a sort of Yankee-millwright-
Byzantine—and half listened as the rabbi
Droned intently about the glorious miseries
Of what he liked to call with a proud flourish
Of possessiveness—"our people." Boring.

If you sucked Necco wafers very slowly
A whole hour somehow would expire.
You had no patience for bygone fate.
Dark eyes, dark hair, olive smolder of skin,
Your ardor couldn't help but loathe
Such parroting—a language no one spoke,
Impossible names, the coy Tetragrammaton,
And the awe you were bound to fabricate.

God seemed more emptiness than presence,
A well run dry, a motto voiced too often.
And what did such might have to do with women?
Were you to bleed and swell in order
To kneel and praise men's grievous certainties?

You sat in the factory town where looms
Once thrummed ceaselessly,
Where the delicate hands of children, some
Younger than you, flew like mechanical birds
And where in the now-archaic buildings
Shafts of dusty light described time's demise.

The afternoon trudged on—a caravan in a sandstorm.
The little rabbi insisted, pleaded, orated,
His gait wobbly with millennial weight.
Soon, you would have a new body,
Soon, you would leave the pale singsong of childhood,
And you dreamt, as dusk fell and cars crept by,
Of that ancient, godless flowering.

Eve Dying

The foretaste flared in a bleak twitch—
A memory that couldn't be,
Her final heart flinching.
She threw the caging clothes aside

And fled her housed duties
While overhead
A cold cloud glowered,
The grimace of gathered nullity.

Womb-ruined, a stone
In her dwindled voice, fast
Fear shaking the seed
Of first faith while the sour

Coffin of breathless power
Prepared its lone line—
The only god-promise
She could not conceive.

Her staggered, shortened moans
Smashed every fable
She had been told.
Time shrank to a groan.

Imagine her stretched out
Upon the ground—horizon
And sky resolutely empty.
No painter appears or apostle.

When the jackals draw near
They sniff and begin to cry,
Their voices plangent, raw—
Less and more than human.

Millions

Last week I called two guys to get bids
On cutting down a maple near the end of the driveway.
One guy came in at five-fifty, the other at six-fifty
But he agreed to five-fifty after I told him
What the other guy quoted me. The job involved
Dropping some massive limbs thirty feet up, chipping
The brush and cutting the trunk into manageable pieces
That I then can saw up for firewood.
Lawrence Summers, a famous guy who will fall
Into the vat of oblivion with the passing of time,
Made five point two million last year for advising
A hedge fund. He worked one day a week so we
Can assume his advice was more than "buy low, sell high."
Everything has a price. Look at slavery auctions
Or the reservoir down the road that was built
In the Thirties when the power company decided
To dam a modest lake and generate electricity.
When I talk with the guy from the tree service company
He complains that his chipper is getting old and he'll have
To buy a new one soon. "There goes my profit," he laments.
Lawrence Summers is all profit, a trough everyone
Would like to feed at except for a few poets
Who have mastered the trick of living solely on oxygen
And don't need to use money. When a ten-dollar check
Comes in the mail for a poem they laugh and use it
To start a fire in the Jøtul of blow-down—
Wood that lived its life without any cash whatsoever,
That grew from random seeds that blew on the wind
That right now riffles through the thinning hair
Of the tree cutter who takes his baseball cap off

And says how beautiful the view is from our hillside.
We look at the view, then shake hands. I go in the house
And look up the hedge fund that Lawrence Summers
Worked for but they aren't taking deposits of breath.

Bob Dylan (Chile, 1973)

Footfalls   their sound
Deliberate   and indifferent.
A metal   door.
A smell   like burnt hair.
A table   and   two chairs.

We know who you are.
We know you go around
And you play the songs of this gringo,
Bob Dylan.

A soldier   making a face
Like eating   something rotten.

We wonder why you do that.
We wonder why you insult your country.
Your country is your mother.
Don't you love your mother?

As if   searching   for an answer
The lieutenant   looked at a wall   carefully.

You are fortunate.
We have a guitar here and we want you to play.
We will be your audience, Mister Mother Hater.
Some people say that soldiers are stupid, cruel people
But they are wrong. We are aficionados.

His fingers were wood   his voice   a dark whisper.
They stared   with dead smiles   on their faces.

For as long   as he could   he made the song go on
As if   it were a train   that could take him away.
A sergeant   came over   and grabbed the guitar,
Held it by   its neck and smashed it   to the floor.

There is the wind's answer, señor.
There are your words, señor.
The good Americans are helping us.
Your name was given us by another musician.
We have our own instruments.

A stick   came   toward his privates.
He felt   the blue scream   of electricity.
When he   woke he was lying in a field.
The air was   cold.
It   was night.
Was he   still   a person?
His teeth   chattered   like impatient dice.
His eyes   felt severed   from their sockets.

In his mind   he saw   the American girl
Who had been   his lover   that year in the States.
She made love when   she wanted,
She ate   when   she wanted,
She said   what   she wanted.
They   had heard   Dylan sing.
It was startling so much poetry   in his anger.

He tried   to rise   but his legs were sand,
He curled up   as best   he could
And started   to cry   like a lost child,
A child who feels   he never   will see home again,
Who   is full   of the worst woe.

He thought of her   and tried   to imagine the tongue
Of love   in his mouth.   Such a sweet snake.
In his gut   a pain like   a turning blade.
He   wished to   throw up.

In his mind   he saw a man   walking down
A quiet street   toward   a woman's house.
It was dusk   there was   a light fragrant wind.

He sang a song   that   could not be unlearned.

for Owen

On a Photograph by Dorothea Lange

Idle as fate,
The sheriff tips his chair back
And surveys the blank
Amiable ground
Of his Oklahoma town.

The law nods.
He, the victor, yawns.
Phlegmatic, prone
To leer at nothingness,
He was born to this estate

That separates the human race
From bedazzled anarchy.
Fear tiptoes by. Respect
Doffs its stupid hat.
The sheriff spits

A wad of something
At the surd of emptiness.
He waits and doesn't:
The all-too-human
Tends to the criminal.

Some unrequited sage
Will kill
The pangs of love.
Colored and white will leak
Historic rage.

Fat with peace,
He can ignore the horizon's
Vast ethereal spite.
He can abide
As if darkness held light.

Florida

Dutifully she lies in bed but cannot sleep.
One night a searching hand will reach into
Her small, plain room with the photos of
Grandchildren on the walls and one of her
Late husband on the three-drawer dresser.

No sounds outside the condo's walls, no living
Sounds within—the cat died up north.

                                        Cancer.

But watching death isn't like doing it.
She lies there and tries to fret about dollars
Or doctors or daughters-in-law but her mind
Keeps lapping at the shore of her body.

Sometimes she feels contempt for some woman
In the grocery who announces while plucking
A liter of diet soda where she is going next.

"What do you know?" she wants to yell.
"Who the hell do you think you are, a prophet?"

She thinks of other photographs, the women
In long dark dresses, the men in gabardine.
America prefers the cheerful colors.
Everyone extols orange juice,
A strange flavor she has never grown used to.

She should rend her clothes and tear her face,
Make a brutal sight of her long-enduring self.
She should stand in front of the vast plate-glass window
Proclaiming bargains and wail like regret
To the suntanned women and their autos.

The photos convict her—*Kinder* in sundresses
And shorts, a handsome man on his wedding day,
Old women who once lay in beds of their own
Beneath a Baltic sky of heedless stars.

She has forgotten the rationales for murder.
Here, who could believe there lived a Hitler?

The refrigerator wheezes,
A punctual mechanical companion hosting
A packaged cornucopia. What has she become,
She wonders, that the sound gives her comfort?

Ode to Time

If you'd been a writer in the 40s and 50s
You'd have drunk and smoked yourself to an early death.
"Another Manhattan, Gus."
"Damn, I'm out of Luckies."
Hard living would have agreed with you.
So what if death made suitable arrangements?
To your children you would bequeath matchbooks with
    advertisements:
Cure hemorrhoids, Study at home, Collect exotic stamps.

You get to be born later
And eat a bran muffin for breakfast each day
With organic grapefruit juice to wash it down.
Plus you shovel in vitamins to keep nutritionally shipshape.
Your blood is gorgeous.
Bacteria weep over you.
You'll get to sit around the assisted living facility
And make bets as to who will go next.
You'll get to talk about your bowel movements
And grind your teeth, which aren't in bad shape
Considering your advanced age,
About another Republican president
Who squares morality with greed and smiles about it.
His teeth are in good shape, too.
One hundred years earlier he would have run a railroad
And used up human lives like Kleenex.
Maybe there weren't Kleenex then—an anachronism,
Time's hiccup.

Time doesn't exist but is real.
It took billions of years for the planet to make it this far.

That's why people binge.
There's a lot to take in:
"Give me another Old-Fashioned."
"I'd like to go to bed with you, Sharon."
"I'd like to go to bed with you, Tom."
Time is a polluted, ugly river.
Sorrow rains for days, the banks overflow.
Corpses bob on the waters.

"Human material," the Communists called it.
They were cynical, brutal, scientific.
In 1850 they would have been tethered to an estate
And spent their days scything buckwheat.
They would have worn embroidered shirts and praised
    God.
In 1935 they build hydroelectric plants and despise God
As not even a notion.
Permanent Futurists, they have risen in Time's ranks.

All this applies to you because the morning the planes hit
You were at the doctor's dealing with an earache.
Where did that come from?
You swallow supplements like a Eucharist that is going out
    of style.
It is going out of style but you get to live anyway.
Fifty years earlier you would be wearing a gray flannel suit
And plotting another adultery.
Your building would never fall down.
You say the word because you like it—"never."

After work you would stand on the sidewalk,
Breathe in the intoxicating exhaust and wonder
Which bar and grill tonight, which dame to call:
"Look, Gladys, I been thinking.

We were good in the sack together."
At your wing-tipped feet
A dark wind blows scraps of tabloids—
Time whistling.

for Howard Levy

Indelible

"I'm Hungry for Love"
The disc on the old phonograph announces.
It could be Billie Holiday, the imperfect lady.
Immaculately a voice of coffee and honey
Swings each uncoated, impenitent note.

Down the halls and streets
Radios writhe with bleating innocence,
The spun sugar of first love,
But in shadowy, late-afternoon rooms
Desire moans for what it has lost,
Or worse, not known.

Long fingers light a cigarette, unkissed lips
Blow smoke arabesques as if to evoke
A heaven where each round sensation
Left the skeptic mind behind
To float in the myth of assured emotion—
As if this hurt could be kind.

The scattered valentines that adorn
The record jacket are bittersweet blue.
The sax strews flatted harmony.

A man and woman drift, engage, drift.
They linger in night-silence
As if a tune were beseeching them.
A cool contentment seeps in as they
Entwine fingers, kiss sleepily—happy animals.

Later, on the subway, at work,
They review that sinuous patter,
Hum the delectable chords
While far beyond the day-lit buildings
The musical body quivers.

for Sherry

II

Goya's Instructions

Before the stench is vicious
Sketch the corpses
Where the bomb has visited,
Where limbs and torsos roost
Obediently
And the vitals lie open
To frank but harmless light.

Resist the impulse of simile.
Art instructs us
To linger in the present.
Human hands assembled
These deaths. Stained
Fingers remain beautiful.
Blame God for dexterity.

Resist, too, the camera's
Encompassing wisdom.
Mark by eager mark
Ferret this disaster—
The hand's best work
Is to feel like the blind
Through the fog of suffering.

Do not fret. Do not turn
Away. Later there
Will be the valedictions
Of flowers and creeds.
Cries and wails will shred
The air but loss cannot
Be summed. Draw, then,

So line can fashion
Feeling. What is blank
Can be contoured in black.
No priest can undo
This stubborn vision.
On that half face there—
The effigy of a grin.

High Fidelity

"Listen to this," Lester, my mother's boyfriend
(A stupid term since Lester was bald
And in his mid-forties), enthused. "It's
High fidelity." He put on one of those stringed plagues—
Mantovani—he favored and assumed a gaze
That signaled techno-cultural rapture.
I liked the truncated phrase, though—"hi fi."

I was mired in my late boy's life,
Rooting for an embarrassing ball team
And watching my mother appoint another
Loveless duplex in her plastic-slip-covers taste
While the blank-eyed bunny hop of progress
Fomented on fronts I couldn't conceive.

Men and women in white laboratories
Were hatching the brisk perfection of high fidelity;
I was dreaming of fingers reconnoitering
Nancy Smith's breasts, softly stimulating those darlings.

"How do you like it?" Lester asked.
I answered with my standard "great" that showed
Without prevarication how much I loathed him.
"I like the music too," and paused, "sort of."

Lester smiled a nasty, rueful smile
That meant I should absent myself lest
Violence ensue. More often than not I stayed
And welcomed his screaming and throwing things.

Spittle leapt from his mouth—so much excited spume.
If my mom was present she started whimpering.
The Theme from Some Movie swelled, then lapsed,
The perfect soundtrack for empty indignity.

Fantasia on Three Sentences
from a Letter by Robert Lowell

Elizabeth is finishing her novel.
I'm teaching Homer.
My car won't start in the snow.

If I drank less, I'd turn
Into an amiable bore,
Take up golf, scan the *Times*
As if it meant something to me personally.

Achilles is the name of our
Neighbor's cocker spaniel.
He sits at the window and yaps
At Helen's fraught ghost.

Novels are the aspirin of
Diminished possibility;
Narrative is the condom
Of optimism.

        Don't I love
To make pronouncements!
Yesterday I bit down on a candy bar
And broke a tooth.
Not a bad scene with which
To start a novel:
"Not particularly out of sorts
For a permanently *louche* nincompoop
Arthur bit down on a Baby Ruth
And felt a molar on the left side
Of his mouth moan."

Why do people clean out their cars?
Mine is cozy with candy wrappers,
Library books and loose cigarettes.
I could nest there,
A zero at the end of a large number.

I would prefer to reside in an era where,
While snow sighs,
No one sits on a cold seat
And tries by turning a small key
To coax a heap of metal
Into petrol-swigging life.

The snow descends on our car
Like a hopeless benediction,
Like the Pope granting Kafka an audience,
Like God stockpiling peace,
Like the boredom of angels.

Coughing like a minor character
With an endearing patronymic,
Time's rigor sputters to life,
A weary war horse,
A De Soto with a faulty muffler
Chauffeured by Hector who is wiping
The frosty windshield with a gloved hand
And looking for the corner of Eighth
And Continuity.

Evenings

The sort of man always announcing plans,
Then plodding off to take a nap.
"There's worse," his wife once said without
Sullenness, as if love lay in avoidance.

Futility rises as well as anyone in the morning.
It's evenings that are brown, restless hells,
That crumble like plaster and faint like ghosts.
I see him in his tee shirt on the porch next

To our porch, a glass of ice water in his hand.
Moths swarm the yellow bulb above his head.
The TV chuckles inside. He asks me how I am
And starts talking about how much jack he could

Have made if only he'd gotten a chance.
I listen awhile, then excuse myself. He wags
A finger and asks if I'm too good for him.
I start to speak but already he's turned away.

for William Wallace

Sestina for a National Security Advisor

Before you deplane, the eternal questions
Recur: "Is your tie cinched and your fly zipped?"
Once in Moscow an assistant winced
And you got it. You were, after all, brilliant;
Statesmen, editors, and starlets
Agreed. If there were dissenters, a joke

Told at your expense that made a joke
Of them sufficed. Who were they to question
Someone who'd trafficked with starlets,
The shade of Bismarck, and numerous unzipped
Eminences? "It's lights that are brilliant,
Henry, not people," a prof counseled. You winced

And when it rained more bombs, Harvard winced:
Ever-practical Death offered no jokes.
Televised talking heads proffered brilliance
To echo yours though the mortal questions
Left cavalier wit spewing the colloquial *zip*.
Thank the gods of gossip for the décolletage of starlets:

"Henry the K Cozies Up with Starlet!"
Tabloid glitz that made Foggy Bottom wince—
Jealous, dry martini twerps. You zipped
It up and went back to the Borscht Belt jokes
You slayed the Middle East with, the fawning questions
You tossed Nixon whose answers were brilliant

Or so you assured him. You were loyal—as brilliant
A ploy as the slyest, bed-hopping starlet
Ever devised. When he called in the night with questions

About himself, you felt the darkness in your room wince:
Who could tell where ambition ended and a joke
Began whose quiet, ghastly ironies zipped

Past the news magazines, pundits, and zip-
Headed hipsters and into the perfidy of brilliance?
Alas, the president was an unsteady joke
And no amount of football, beer, and starlets
Could keep those in the printed know from wincing:
Noisy democracy must have its questions.

If shuttles meant zip to a pouting starlet
Stroking your brilliance, at least she didn't wince
At your jowly jokes. And she undid all questions.

for Richard Hoffman

The hitchhiker

I pick up in New Sharon says
He's popping Percocet like M&M's.
Worked on bridges, hurt his back.
Twisted it like a stressed strut.

Seen docs, pt's, even a lady who stuck
Hot needles in him.
They tell you it's gonna work and you believe 'em
Because what are you gonna do?

Snowless, ugly, brown January outside.
Trees waiting, grass waiting, rivers frozen.
What's the point of this? He blurts it,
More to the windshield than to me.
Repeats it more loudly,
Starts drumming two fingers on the dash:
Pitta pat, pitta pat, pitta pat.

Ummm, I twitter like a broken radio,
Turn toward him, shake my head wearily,
A brimming, perplexed offering.
Kindness knots my throat like bile.

Shit, he says, then smiles halfheartedly.
I can't bend over to shoot eight ball.
Here I am livin' on earth—
He pauses, looking at himself through words--
And I can't shoot eight ball. I was a king.

I stop the headshaking, stifle a dazed scream,
Mumble about logs on the pulp truck
Before us, breathe out fatalist
Bacilli from my own soggy soul.

Outside the drugstore
That's advertising specials on Corona and Oreos
We say goodbye. *If you know someone*
Who needs a fucked-up welder, I'm the man.

Limps off, door closes, car moves, sky trembles—
A deep, insouciant blue.

The Novel of Alcohol

After the clamor of invention subsided—
The spurious heat of the authoring self,
The brittle arrogance of insight,
The brooding that makes an honest book—
There was the bottle.
Typically misrepresented by those
Who believe in the duty of meaningful works
That amber fire mimed for an hour or two
The greater awakening, the personal sun
That once rose so spectacularly
To quicken the veins of the stoniest morning.

That, too, subsided into complaint, silence,
A listing belligerence that amused some
Of the locals on the plaza and bored the rest.
"The great gringo"—another fool, more or less.
Still, those onlookers rarely pursed their lips.
They had their own ruined gods
And grasped in their calm way, the whole
Sorriness of the artist's volcanic light. Bound
To flicker and faint, they might have said.
Bound in its Odyssean urge to visit too soon
The uncanny land of the wordlessly dead.

Talking Mrs. Carbone Blues

Buried in the sixth paragraph it says that Mrs. Carbone,
The soldier's mother, feels that "my son shouldn't have
    been there."
The article already has explained in reasonable detail that
Her son was part of a convoy, that someone shot an RPG,
And that this someone was, according to intelligence
    sources,
"From a cellular organization."

When you think about it, Mrs. Carbone, war
Gets way too much press to begin with.
Forty thousand go down on the highway each year.
Sixteen thousand are variously shot to death, knifed,
    bludgeoned, choked.
Whatever lethal mayhem you can imagine is likely
Being perpetrated at this mundane moment.

War gets a lot of press because the cost-per-death ratio is
    high,
The rhetoric curve is steep, the prez-posturing-
For-the-photographers-on-the-flight-deck factor is
    irresistible.
But your son died so you would have the right
To mouth off in paragraph six.
That's no small thing. How many reporters showed up
To talk to moms in Rwanda or Bosnia or Kosovo
Or East Timor or—you get the picture.

Freedom needs security to be freedom, otherwise it's
That existential, loosey-goosey, enjoy-life-today
Kind of freedom that doesn't sit well with

The Protestant baggage that wants salvation,
Innocence and SUV's at the same time.
Freedom is vigilance; freedom is kicking some retributive
     butt.

It's summer and there's probably some blood on the wall
From where you swatted a mosquito or two.
You sit in your apartment and stare at the stain
And your son Timmy's picture in a fake gold frame
On the mantel over the fireplace that doesn't work.

Don't go there, Mrs. Carbone, don't be thinking.
Don't freak people out when they ask how you are doing.
Ask them if they heard about that accident last night
On Route 136. Say that it's too bad about all these
     accidents.

For Leo

in memoriam, L. C.

I can see his ego huffing up the hill
Of another unrecognized day.

His genius was sad; he was sad; the whole
Bleeding delirious planet was sad
But could be happy if they acknowledged him—
If not as the poet to swallow all poets—
At least as righteous usurper of whatever
Miserable academic toss-pot of a crown
Was there for the vatic taking.

How he hated those who prospered
In poetry's well-groomed fields, who never
Deigned to throw his way the gilded crumb
Of a grant or gig, much less the chortling review
Intimating that a condo on Parnassus
Was only a matter of sibilant time.

                        Not for him—
The most ungainly, the most bumptious,
The one who elbowed his way to the empty table,
The one who called out "Death" at the wedding,
"Fate" at the mildest accident, "Desire" at
The rise of a dozy prick, the one who knew
The lower rungs upside down, who had
The feckless temerity to be a sidewalk-pounding,
Hot-enough-for-you, how-you-doin' salesman,
The caller of attention to the wart of money,

The Un-Cool, Talk-Your-Ear-Off, Robert-Browning-
Quoting, Larger-Than-Art Romantic.

                                              Bad manners,
Bad breath, bad heart, he was the one you
Hoped to forget, the one who amounted
To an ever uneven sum, the last, first
And in-between poet, the too too real one.

A Visitation (1968)

Dude—tall, vegetarian thin,
Hasn't had a steak ever,
Clear, watery blue eyes
That don't look through you
Because you can't believe they're
Seeing anything they're so pale—
Dude shows up in the evening—
Before midnight—
Says he knows so-and-so who knows
So-and-so
And he's got
In any case
Some Mary Jane and he's willing
To offer a sample
And we're not looking around
Too many corners because we've
Figured the universe is quaking
Plasma anyway
So our opinions,
Outlooks and forecasts
Are the jive
The ego tells itself
To high-five
The anxious dark
Which is to say
That to tutored eyes
He doesn't look like a narc.

He fires up a fat spliff,
Passes it around and I get
That earnest doper vibe from this cat,

One of those for whom the herb
Is the First Church of the Metaphysical Thirst.

He has on a sort of white linen
Sailor blouse and I told you about the eyes
And he looks a little otherworldly
Even before I inhaled what turned out
To be some quality weed—
You know, two hits and you're floating
Over whatever walls your mind has erected—
The glum shit of your past,
Your parents, your body—
You're transcending, which is why
The whole thing is against the law.

When I ask the guy his name, he says
In a light, high voice as though he's been
Doing nitrous since the fifth grade,
"Shelley, Percy Bysshe Shelley"
And I say "that's an old-fashioned name"
Because that's all the thinking I'm capable of
And he smiles and leans back on the ratty couch
And says he heard about us and wanted
To check it out—the Dead on the stereo,
"The unfettered breasts" (his phrase),
The shimmering kiss of the Day-Glo anima.

"You know," he says, "here is here.
You might as well dig it"—and similar
Dope wisdom, which is cool because we're all
Spacing out real sweetly and he's with the flow—
No need to pull poetry out of his back pocket
And wow us with words, no need to get between
The mind and its sensory gift-wrapping.

                    When, toward dawn, he split,
He left a phone number that I called
Some days later, looking to score and hang out,
But what I got was a Chinese restaurant
Offering two-for-one chow mein.

Had we been prone to wondering, we might
Have searched further but we weren't and didn't.
Spirits fell from the sky regularly.
Each lost day exhumed eternity.

The Uses of Literature

Even at midnight it remained too hot to sleep
And I was weary of chugging beer

That I sweated out as soon as I swallowed.
Not good for anything but *Paradise Lost* –

My favorite poem, any book would do the trick.
I craved decibels and read for the hectoring joy of it.

Hot, though, in Texas beyond the wiles of rhetoric.
I wondered, as I liked to do, how I would act

In Adam's and Eve's flesh if I were they.
Free will is spiritual Jell-O wrestling but

Maybe, as the original dharma plowboy, I
Could have changed the dismal course of human agency.

Beelzebub is ranting. Hard to find a calm word
In the whole infernal poem. Anger and remorse, anger

And remorse. Still, I don't rise to fetch another Lone Star.
This stagnant funk isn't the worst of fallen states.

I swear I feel a breeze and sense a simile
Coming over me, an archangel's impossible face.

for Robert Cording

III

The Torture Channel

I want to watch the Torture Channel.
I am tired of regular violence—
Cops shooting hapless criminals,
Then kicking the corpse with a look
That is half sad-eyed, half gratified
Or savoring an *aperçu*
About mortality—death being little more
Than a prepositional phrase
Appended to the free verse of life.

I hear there are cameras in Guantánamo.
I want to see the blindfolds,
The prods, the underwater tank,
The rods for orifices.
I am paying for it.
Right now a plane is aloft
With a body or two in a bag.
The bag is alive and being delivered.
"Here is a terrorist.
We Westerners
Are not so stupid after all
Nor squeamish."
In certain quarters this garners respect.

I want to see the torturers.
Women do it too—gender equity.
I am safe to watch television
But it doesn't have all the channels.
There should be a Poetry Channel
Where I read my poems

In a voice of pained frivolity
Or deranged seriousness.
It might be torture to people
Who only watch crime shows.

Some of the Nazi *Kommandanten* read
Lyric poetry—purity of race and language
Being no strangers to one another.
A few big-time torturers were hanged
After the war; most willing executioners
Put their evil in a drawer and shut it—
An exciting episode that got bad reviews.

It is still in there,
Smirking and simpering,
Offering rationales, masking
Boredom and anger, wringing out
Fear's dark droplets. Sometimes I think
I hear it at night when the TV is off.

It sounds very thin and far away,
Almost like music or a voice
With a broken windpipe.

Chinatown

She let someone in and someone capped her.
One of the detectives is a woman
Who won't let the guys flatter
Their sexist assumptions.

The detectives drink coffee—typically
One sugar, one half-and-half.
Tastes like one-way love, tastes like no clues,
Tastes like Monday, tastes like black fog.

"Postmodernism is the opiate of the self-conscious."
The cops could grasp that graffito because they live
In the Victorian century, the 'hood of brusque
Honesty and inward complicity. They sort

Out perps the way Darwin and the bishops did
But hit the same walls. They can't miss the sprayed
Sprawl: NO-GOD RULES, JESUS GOT BALLS.
Dubious purpose keeps offing witnesses.

In Chinatown a chieftain downs a cocktail
Of powdered roots and vodka. Women are a mistake
He cultivates. Vanity is smooth as his long hair
But his temper is a wandering trigger.

"Did she deserve to die?" The woman detective
Is shouting. The guys look down at their shoes.
Explanations are the handcuffs on rage,
But blood is louder—blood laughs at the pain.

My Bands

1. The Pimples

If we called attention to our lowly selves
Did that dissolve those selves
Like existential Alka-Seltzers?
We hoped parody would grow up
And turn into a crotch-thrusting headliner,
The right, girl-beckoning stuff.

Meanwhile, we liked the notion of our Fenders
And our so-called playing them more
Than the wroth truth of trashing one meek chord
After another. "Zits, zits, zits"—
Our voices chirped like chipmunk castrati.

At random moments, we produced a sub-musical rumble
That verged on the Liverpool-gone-Southern-
States twang we believed we were up to.
When a song was over, we looked at
One another imploringly: are we there yet?
Will our deafness orchestrate genius?
It was fun because our 'rents considered it
"A constructive use of leisure time" and it wasn't.

2. No Brain No Gain

Chick singer in a black leather halter
And five pounds of eye shadow.
She was beyond sexy though it
Was too dark at the typical gig

To say where that was.
Afterwards we waited for her
To change while we sat on our amps
And nursed the night's transfusion.

On stage, she yelled in her fake Brit accent:
"You poor arses aren't pros!"
We were, though, a fair match,
She hating the prefigured poise of words,
We hating the sheen of glib notes,
All of us seeking
A punk hara-kiri, a distortion orgasm,
In-a-gadda-de-Dada,
The Great Lost Screaming God of Hendrix *WahWah*.

One night she didn't leave her backstage den
But we didn't bother to knock—
Soon she'd emerge to our ironic cheers.
When the bouncer stove the door in
She remained on her chair, a drooping flower
With a small barb in her.
The dim yet fluorescent morgue made
The sort of skin-crawling sense we craved.

3.   Heartbound

"Everybody goes country at some point,"
A worldly wise barfly in Tampa
On his fourth rum and Coke once informed me.
Must be the desire that hides in every guitar—
Let me go to Nashville and cry.
Must be the Chet Atkins twang that resonates
Into honky-cowboy-outer-space.

Must be the grievance of growing old on the road—
A stale room at two in the forsaken morning.

Though we warbled to the shit-kicking moon
We had the funk licks
That bubbled up from the paleo-blues lagoon,
The pedal steel thick as old engine oil,
Our voices wise-ass mournful—harmonies
For the Weary Church of the Unrepentant,
Salvation's sweet listless tune.

Our long-time soundman, Jody, thought we were
Something Dylan might have conjured—
The empty six-pack of American wanting,
The magnolia mansion's shot-out panes,
The two-lane blacktop through West Don't-Explain.
We broke up in the middle of a second set
When our drummer, Pee Wee, put down
His sticks and announced to the six people
In the audience and the bored bartender,
"This sucks."
We nodded to one another, relieved.

4. Al and the Allies

Since there was no "Al," we took turns at it.
"Who's Al tonight?" we'd ask. Occasionally
We asked an Al in the audience to sit in with us.
We'd disappeared years ago anyway
In the tunnel of hard notes, the didn't-I-
Hear-you-guys-before life and times
And, blinking, emerged with the riffs
We began with, the father hoard

Of Bo, John Lee and Chuck
They were wont to brag about—rightly so—
To journalists in the High Sixties
Who sought the Black Origins of the White Noise.

We stood very still and let our callused fingers talk
And some nights it happened—maybe
Someone looked up from his or her beer, maybe not—
But we were in the baby-shake-that-red-dress groove,
The one that blew away the sorry details
Of who our skins were and where they were going
And what we thought and what we forgot
In a smooth long paroxysm that was
In Jimmy the Bassist's words, "Better than sex."

No millions of dollars
And no letting go of the bad habits
We'd acquired along the blown amp way.
That was okay.

for Tim Seibles

Flares

Going off over
The garage. Incoming.
Dark and quiet in the house.
Dog on the braided

Rug Marlene made
Back in the 70s.
Shifts in his sleep.
McAllister screams:

"Help me!"
Night dark and quiet.
President speaking.
Which one?

Democracy and freedom.
Incoming.
Marlene left the rugs
When she left.

"I still love you but. . . ."
Freedom. Night dark.
Flares going off. Screaming
In his blood.

Dog picks his head up.
Democracy.
Middle of the night.
Quiet. Incoming.

Heptonstall Cemetery

You can take the short tour—
    birth date, education,
    cataclysmic meeting,
    marriage, literary lightning,
    ghastly death, posthumous myth—

Or the *pas de deux*—
    quotes from Shakespeare (a weapon
    they loved to point at themselves),
    a crumpled map of indirection
    drawn by a pocked gypsy,
    diaries of gloom and euphoria—
    bumptious America and occult England mating,
    the stereopticon of rivaled ambition.

You can reflect on how
    they wove the taut weft of the self
    with the ghost of the un-self,
    how they visioned their souls as peers
    in a vaunting, half-lit drama,
    the last, blood-orange shivers of feeling,
    how the protean earth was a stage
    but the page a truer one.

You can stand in the late, seeping, winter light
    and huddle against the cold,
    look about you for a fox or hare,
    listen for a woman's surprised laughter.

You can kneel on the frozen ground
  and imagine the underworld
  and how poets pass back and forth,
  back and forth in their blind intuitions.

You can walk back in the dark, shoulders hunched,
  a great weight made palpable
  in this coming to the end of words,
  this lingering for as long as you can stand to linger
  and feeling your own pulse become strangely electric,
  as if a prophecy already had occurred.

One morning in California

(Which, in his journals, the skeptical Thoreau noted—
    apropos
Of the forty-niners—was three thousand miles nearer to
    hell)
Two working girls (as they used to call them in my
    neighborhood)
In micro-skirts, halters and platform heels are arguing
About a guy and calling each other unsavory names in the
    lemony
Early morning light on an otherwise empty boulevard
    sidewalk
When one (slightly taller, a brunette) suddenly pulls a small
    knife
Out of her tiny pocketbook and waves it sort of spastically.
The other woman doesn't draw back but throws herself into
    the art
Of vituperation all the more but then—again suddenly—a
    guy has come
Out of a house and he's taken the knife from the woman's
    unsteady hand
And he's patting her on the back and mouthing words along
    the lines of
"It's okay, baby, it's okay," and that seems to be the end of it
But the other woman pulls a knife out of her tiny purse and
    before
You can say "transcendentalist" inserts it into the guy's ribs.
All three scream at once, then the guy starts lurching, the
    knifer woman
Starts to run off as best she can in her absurd shoes, and
    the woman

Who was being comforted starts howling like an abandoned
    dog.

The cop who writes this all down later in abrupt English
Read Thoreau in Humanities One-O-Three, a requirement
    for
A criminal justice degree, but his taste for stoic punditry is
    slaked
By his colleagues whose nose for philosophic obscenity is
    unerring.

No one dies in this altercation and the long-playing record
Goes on like the seasons on earth Thoreau was so keen
    about in his gruff
Yet tender way, with one fresh inevitability following
    another
And the celibate author tramping the byways of Concord
    and paying
Attention to plants, shrubs, insects and birds in the same
    assiduous fashion
That many of his fellow Americans caressed their account
    books.
He never wanted to become a totem of individualism any
    more than
A tree asks to be hit by lightning or a cop asks to be shot by
    some
Raving crackhead.
                Literature gets passed along like a memento
Whose original occasion is eclipsed by the fact of its being
    passed along.

The magical sun topples into the westering ocean and a tall
    thin guy
With a beard that looks like he trims it himself twice a year

Is hunkered down at a coffee-stained folding table
In some social services bunker where he is manning a
    hotline and shaking
His tired but dauntless head and saying, "Now tell me again
    but
A little slower this time." When he puts the phone down,
    he sighs reflexively,
Then pulls a small notebook from his denim jacket in which
    he begins writing:
If hell were a hole, it already would have filled up by now.
And doesn't every working girl know it.

Motel

She stood on the motel balcony that ran
                        The length of the building
and overlooked
A parking lot in front of another anonymous
     Cinder block building, the air gentle
In the quiet three a.m. city.

Your cliché or mine was what she would say
               To her lover in the fresh moments
Of the strewn morning, as if who left
     Whom first mattered rhetorically.
One of us will leap and fall a few sorry feet,
Exclaim, then flick regret's dispensable switch.

She hugged her robed self—
          Within the cool brocade of skin
     An afterglow tingled.
Sex sugared with a moody fraction of love:
          No compound was more astutely impure.

Like a tongue that had never touched
          Another tongue, desire fumbled with the door lock,
Groped for the room light,
          Gaped at the cheap bed.
As any night clerk could vouch,
     There was no good alias.

A few lights on across the way—others still at it.
She felt drowsy, then found herself smiling—
          Not out of bliss but fondness.

The Army-Navy Game

This feels as eternal as anything in America—
An inevitably gray December day,
The thermometer a few wan degrees above freezing.

I perch on the living room couch
(The cushions are shot; my body feels weirdly weightless)
Waiting for my mom to get herself ready
To visit the kindly implacable doctor.

Though I can't throw a football fifteen yards
With anything like accuracy, I know this game
Is played every year and it's conceivable that I,
As yielding human stuff, could be on that field
Or in the band blowing a cold trumpet.

The announcers talk about bragging rights
And servicemen all over the world.
They talk with some old guys who used to be young guys.

When I go upstairs to check on my mom,
Who should have come downstairs by now,
I find her lying on the floor softly crying.
Her walker is down there beside her.
She's on her side staring up at me as if
I were a cloud or the top of a tree.
Her eyes are small. Her lipstick is smudged.
Her hair is sparse.

I bend over and start to hoist her up
But she's heavy as grief.

Downstairs the TV chatters on.
I could be there in Philadelphia yelling
With wholesome excitement but I'm here
Propping pillows under my mother and positioning
A chair for her to grab onto and hearing her quaver that
She would as soon be dead.

Her voice is high and thin,
Weary of its body.

I'm young but sympathize.
I forfeited my ration of eternity as a kid
Playing football in the backyard:
Come nightfall, Stevie Schwartz and I
Kept heaving our ardor through the black air.

It sounds as though someone has scored a touchdown.
I've got my mom up onto a chair.
She's stopped crying. I'm grateful.
Oh, Army-Navy-December-football-cancer-afternoon life,
I, too, should start cheering.

"My Son Has a Persistent Qualitative Motor Disorder"

Oh, she was the mother of that catastrophe:
Her child a spindly hurricane, misshapen boat,
A broken spark of resolute energy
Yet a body named in Christian charity,
Yet the call of her cells, her own hard notes.

Oh, she was the mother of that catastrophe—
The boy gurgling a shard of music happily,
The boy much more (she knew) than clinical rote.

A broken spark of resolute energy,
If he was ever-lost, he was still he,
A bottom soul whose flesh noisily spoke.

Oh, she was the mother of that catastrophe,
The soil of what flamboyantly disagreed
With sense, what asked to be loved without hope,
A broken spark of resolute energy
That never would explain what it could see,
The palpable animal that shook and groped.

Oh, she was the mother of that catastrophe,
A broken spark of resolute energy.

Taxi

Sometimes they don't want to talk.
You are full of good feeling—
On your way to a tryst or surrounded
By comforting packages or suffused
With the soft fiery lift of distilled spirits
But the driver spits at the motioning lights,
Twists the steering wheel petulantly.

Sometimes they do talk—their native realms.
They have fled famine, inquisition, decades doused in war.
They have fled barren women
And women who gave them children.
They have fled a threadbare shirt,
One pair of exhausted shoes
Yet amid the hard words are trees and flowers,
The buried scents of childhood beckoning.
Suddenly, right there in the cab, they mimic a bird—
Whit whit woo, whit whit woo.
You start,
Perhaps you should make sounds too.
Instead, you listen politely,
Then explain where you are from.
In your backyard cardinals nest in the elderberries.

Sometimes they don't want to talk,
So you read the driver's name
But aren't sure how to pronounce it.
There are too many vowels
Or there are marks over consonants that make no sense.
The man in the ID photo is not smiling.

You wish to imagine the grace of his joy
But the bruise of loss intrudes.

Sometimes they say that this
Is not what it's like back home.
America has more cars, they say,
Many, many more new cars.
They lift their hands from the wheel for a second,
Gesture with them—palms up—to indicate how much
Yet never enough.

Babe Ruth and Kid Rilke

What you doin' there, Kid,
Throwin' pennies down the well of the universe?

Kid Rilke looked up from his labors at the pensive Babe.
O Sultan of Metaphor, how is it you performed

Feats of such heroic, physical exuberance only
To wobble like hope and fall ingloriously?

Ain't that the truth, but you know as well as me
Death's always warmin' up in the bullpen.

Hell, you can get knocked out in the first inning.
Kid Rilke nodded and stretched panther-like.

I tend to go in for metaphysical suppleness
But I like your style, Babe.

You are America, the kinetic expletive,
And I, Europe, the burdened sensualist.

The Babe bit on his hot dog and told
The Kid not to get discouraged: words only

Mattered to sad sacks and fuddy-duddies.
Thanks, the Kid said as the ungainly god

Trotted away. The sky froze to a lachrymose gray.
The Kid sang. The Babe never looked back.

IV

Winning

"We're still winning," Rick's dad said to me
While Rick and his mom were cleaning dishes in the
    kitchen.
I knew he was baiting me about 'Nam
But didn't know why. I nodded abstractedly
And started talking football.
                              It was Thanksgiving,
The day the family salutes the notion of family
And I was invited as Rick's college roommate.
Rick, who was gay, told me he was going to tell
His folks officially and wanted someone straight
To be there to "thin out the flak" in Rick's words.
I sat and listened to Rick's dad who was
In the Air Force and Rick's mom who worked
At the Pentagon tell me about their hobbies:
He assembled model planes and she baked pies.
I admired the models in the glass case that stood
In the living room of their condo and I told
Rick's mom the truth, that I'd never eaten
A better crust in my life.
                            I kept waiting
For something to happen—hysteria, anger, grief—
But we kept eating and going for walks around
The neighborhood and hearing about how even
The smart countries like Israel and Sweden
Respected our fighter planes. On the car trip
Back to school Rick told me it wasn't the right time yet
But it was cool that I came to help out.
We got in an argument about what radio station
To play and I told him he could go fuck himself.

Rick's folks retired to Florida where his dad
Still puts models together and his mom bakes pies.
Rick's been with the same guy for over a decade
And sends me Christmas cards each year
In which he frets about his waist size.

                              I read
That a team of forensic experts is examining skeletons
In Guatemala, Mayans who were massacred around
The time of that Thanksgiving. I was unknowing in one
      sense
And, in another, that I cannot define,
I knew that another haven was going to die.

Cocaine Canto

The possibilities fed by social norms—
    Marriage, a Saab, 1.5 kids—shattered,
    Though not at once in a soap opera storm
Of catty then bitter invective but rather
    In slow motion so that one un-special day
    You notice the cloak of your aims is in tatters.
Metaphor remains a blessed stay
    Against bare facts—1983,
    America enthralled by Reagan le Fay,
A shill for the endangered rights of the wealthy
    But nonetheless an agreeable guy
    And foe of liberals, Reds, and druggies—
The same species to him. He smiled while I tried
    To say "yes" to more freeways, faster food,
    Space weapons orbiting above the sky,
TV's constant pitiless good mood.
    Laugh, laugh. No wonder I sought pleasure
    Not as a circumspect interlude
But as an omni-principle, an armor
    I could buckle on to meet my sometime soul
    When it whined that all I did was serve
My purse. An oblivion I could control,
    One that soothed and piqued the ragged wick
    Of my half-lit life. I loved the whole
Illegal, weirdly comforting schtick—
    I mean the men in cars with casual smiles
    And stolid eyes, I mean the etiquettes
Of usage—excess as a classic style—
    And the vibe that went with it, the stealth
    That cash could buy. I was lost, of course, miles

Away from any semblance of health,
    Mental or otherwise. I could neither sleep
    Nor wake. I longed for the random wealth
Of empty time, those un-high moments sweet
    With being. From my windows I looked at
    People walking down the busy street—
Regular, typical—I loathe those words that
    Narrow the shock a body must feel
    To earn its livid keep. I can't go back
However much I'd wish. I stand revealed—
    A spendthrift who hoarded her desires
    And chose to embrace what was unreal.
I blame no one—the powder was fire
    And I was straw. The twelve-steps that come
    Afterwards leave me uninspired.
The squalor of self-love beckoned. I succumbed.

Shiver

in memoriam, A. C.

Blizzard. First Avenue might be
The yard between Iowa farm house
And barn. The few muffled people
Trudge gingerly in zero visibility:
No rope extends across space
For dire hands to grasp on to.
They totter in the thick swirling air
Like wound-up toys or mummies.

Your high window is a tenuous aerie;
The prolix heart wants and wants
Yet peace comes with the weather—
Nothing doing for a while. The wind
Mourns, then cavorts. Time is purified
Into slow crystals and you think back
To childhood and the incommunicable
Raptures of alertness. You shiver

Though the apartment is steamy warm.
Now the words surface and for a time
The craving is sated in the tingle
And tickle of articulate scratching.
One of the cats jumps onto your table,
As if to say, "Pay attention to me.
I am alive." Disappearing phrases hang
In the darkening sky—mortality's avocation.

Population 4,672

We gazed out the oversized picture window
One gray, forlorn, late autumn afternoon

To see most of the usually pacific mill town
Parading down the two blocks of Main Street.

Cheerleaders kicked and leapt, vaunting legs, breasts, hair,
Chanting, wild with sexual strutting.

The one police car inched along, its blue light blinking,
The rheumatic chief smiling with glad senility.

Skinny football players twirled helmets like lariats
And flashed the V-for-victory sign like generals.

The marching band—perhaps thirteen strong—
Played some ragged, fizzy, pep song.

We had enough emotional firewood to last all winter
As we perched in our bare apartment above

The born-again electrician, across from the funeral home
And next door to the Democrat lawyer.

We who knew who Gandhi, Georgia O'Keefe, Albert
Camus, Ben Webster and Walker Percy were

Had amassed a civilization in our heads.
Surely, we could get this one down.

"Small town," we said to one another
At night as we strolled on the playing field

Behind the high school, peering at the stars
That never seemed so white and far away,

Steering clear of the skunks,
Feeling, at once, intoxicated and sedate.

for Kathy Hooke

Elegy for Paul Butterfield

The blues don't come to you in a mist
No, the blues don't come to you in a mist
The blues come when you dirty and pissed

Et cetera for decades of choruses
As when your whiteness disappears into blankness
As when your darkness stops answering the phone
As when your modest fame goes to cash a small
   check and doesn't return
As when your friends get bored with the plaintive notes
   played too often before

Found dead in your apartment
   That's how it's supposed to be
Oh, found dead in your apartment
   That's how it's supposed to be
If you live the life
   Then it becomes your story

You stood for how long on the burning stage
Blowing and chanting from the throbbing gut
Of pan-racial hoodoo, the appropriated blues
That left you fumbling with the half-life of smack
The black riff of hollow solitude

Love is what's bound to go bad
Say, love is what's bound to go bad
The woman wants what you never had

On the cover of the first album
You stood cool but earnest
As if to say, "This is Chicago."

You couldn't have known
How true the rhymes were,
How the song goes down slow

The Oil Man

The oil man is here, my grandmother announced
In a voice mingling alarm with resignation
And tinged by the asp's tongue of contempt. I always
Marveled at the scabs that had formed over her wounds.
   The oil man is here, my mother announced
In a happy voice that never had been
Shot at or herded into a town square before dawn.
She told my grandmother that this was America.
No one nurtured mourning here.

   The slightly flattened cylinder of the heating oil truck
Has not changed over decades. Any number of wars,
Police actions, skirmishes, ideological vendettas
Have not changed the oil man's squarish, felt cap.

   Every drop of oil is the earth's blood, a sensitive
Girlfriend once told me while I was putting a quart
Into my '64 Ford. Is that good or bad? I asked her.
Sometimes it's hard to make sense of metaphor.
No wonder it largely keeps to poetry.

   I had an Ethical Culture teacher who told us
To beware of anthropomorphism. God was not a person but
A process. Incredibly enough, Mr. Silberman
Had grown up in Shanghai. He was a Taoist Jew,
An incompatibility that seemed to disturb him no more
   than
The oil man is disturbed by the horizon of unrenewable
   finitude
That hovers above the earth like a corona of smog.

The oil man hums while he stands by the hose
He has attached to the tank that is regulated
By the thermostat. Comfort buries imagination and oil is
   oil,
Which is to say the dark tears of oblivion. When a furnace
Turns on, another time-ghost suspires.

My wary grandmother and smiling mother are both gone.
I take the oil man's invoice but say nothing.
The planet gives up its secrets. Every ounce becomes a use.

For His Part: Walt Whitman (1863)

The soldiers in the hospital asked Walt Whitman
    to tell them the story that would
    make the hurt go away, the story about trust and reward.

They knew he knew the story; he was
    a poet and, perforce (as poets once put it),
    belonged to the tribe of the availing Odysseus,
    a voyager in every weather of the soul.

For all his love, he winced. He knew
    the words they wanted and sought to avoid those words.
    He'd been another singer, one from the earth.

The sky was empty and distant. There was no human home
        there.
    It pained him to have to speak that story. He touched
    a forehead, placed a quiet kiss on a pale cheek
    and murmured simple words that caressed the honor of
        their pain,
    the sweetness of the most mangled flesh.

Perhaps they believed the poet. Perhaps for a time the sky
    bowed to the earth, wings became legs, words became
    more than earnest sounds. The poet, for his part, never
    turned away. He saw his poems in the saddest eyes
    and the briefest, most hopeless smiles. The poet voyaged
    to the edge of human warmth and held the hand
    as it turned cold. That was the poem the poet had always
        known
    and from which he never turned away.

DJ (1965)

I lay in bed at night and listened on my transistor.
Radio waves seemed an active miracle and still do:
   I can't believe the silent air brims
      With those chattering arrows.

I was listening to a Negro man: "Greetings, earthlings,
From the big hot boss with the big hot sauce,
The man with the permanent sun tan, the jock
   With no hair, no worldly care,
      Your soul leader, oooh-poppa-dee-der."

Jumping Jesus, I thought to my dizzy self,
   How did a man become a word-motor?
As the Dynamic Daddy-O, Master Metaphor Mixer,
Unblinking Syntactic Flicker of African-American Shtick,
   Trick and No-Trick, he was ultra-bardic.

I lay there softly mimicking him:
The clicking consonants, alto rises and bullfrog plummets,
   The flicking feints and jabs of sex-teasing phrases,
   The long vowels caressed—oooh!—until they seemed
      Like vocal limousines.

If fancy could be translated, the bulwark of Western
   Lit camped beside my bed would have levitated.
I listened till I felt drowsy and hoped I would dream
Of that glowing yet raspy voice, that lovely razor of elocution.

Bud Light

This may be as good a way as any to recall
The well-lit, pre-post-Columbian, let's-get-mellow-
While-the-ecological-bomb-ticks wasteland:
A commercial about a beer that is barely beer,
A thin, refrigerated, almost taste
That seeds a seeping, lurching buzz,
A tumid haze that shambles down the bloodstream
Looking for a loud, laughing oblivion.

It's alcohol masquerading as beer
Which means the commercial presents
A skit about a guy who likes the beer
But is followed into his car and bathroom and office
And even onto a baseball field by a band
Of mariachi players who also like the beer—
Which is funny because they're not American,
Which is funny because they wear funny outfits.
His blonde girlfriend is somewhat put out
Because she wants more from him than bad beer
He thinks is good beer. Still, she's willing to stick
With him because the inference is that a good guy
Who drinks bad beer that he thinks is good beer
Is better than no guy with no beer.
Plus a lot of women drink wine so she's lucky
That the requisite whiff of quiff allows her
To be in the commercial anyway.

The guy is so regular, so brilliantly undistinguished,
He could stand for the stock notion of the nation,
The guy-nation getting up in the morning

And looking in the mirror and saying to himself,
"I'm not going to do that again until
The next time I feel like doing that again."

There's no shortage of ism's to explain
That the comedy isn't funny but outside the commercial
The guy who is buying a twelve-pack at the convenience
     store
On a Wednesday evening isn't listening to why we are
The way we are and how, through words and sincerity,
We could get better. Even as he puts his hard-earned down
On the slightly greasy, Formica counter
He's already sitting in front of the TV
Drinking one beer after another, quickly.

for Maisie

Boys

Your brother died for nothin', Jimbo said
One night over beers to Bobby Rand.
The world goes fuckin' on and he's stayed dead.

Slowly, Bobby raised his spinning head.
Don't talk that shit, don't even think it, man.
Your brother died for nothin', Jimbo said.

I wish there was somethin' else instead;
I wish we were drivin' Billy's old Ford van.
The world goes fuckin' on and he's stayed dead.

I can't go there anymore. I been bled.
Bobby looked down at his sturdy hands.
Your brother died for nothin', Jimbo said.

He didn't die for nothin'. He died for the red
Light above this bar. He died for rock bands.
The world goes fuckin' on and he's stayed dead.

Jillann walked over, winked: *Time for bed,*
Boys. You can dream about your Vietnam.
Your brother died for nothin', Jimbo said.
The world goes fuckin' on and he's stayed dead.

Abandoned Asylum, Northampton, Massachusetts

I stroll the grounds, as a grander era
Would have phrased it, and listen for lost screams.
In the town below, other cries are blasting
The grace of this shy spring afternoon.
I'm here to recall what I never knew.

Broken glass trills softly, wood weeps rot.
I stand on tiptoe and stare through begrimed windows.
The flannel nightshirts are gone, the leather straps
And tubs in which to take cold baths.
A whole hymn-singing century is mouse shit.

I listen for the ghosts of regimens. I listen
For bright eyes throbbing with dolor.
I listen for the taciturn, the bleary, the mopey.
I sit in shadow and await the manna of grief.
Here, the engines of betterment roared

With iron understanding. Here, righteous fear
Practiced on the bent hearts of gasping bodies.
Here, maniac beauty bloomed and declined.
Sumac is growing everywhere like crazy.
I pray to the bricks and splintered casements—*lighten me*.

Acknowledgments

Thanks to the publishers and editors of the following pub-
lications in which some of these poems first appeared: *Agni
Magazine, Paris Review, Face, Rivendell, American Letters
and Commentary, Green Mountains Review, Seneca Review,
Brilliant Corners, St. Petersburg Review, Open City, 5 A.M.,
Iron Horse Literary Review, Prairie Schooner, Wisconsin
Review, Nth Position, Poet Lore, Court Green, Manhattan
Review, Four Corners, U.S. 1 Worksheets, Marlboro Review,
Two Rivers Review, Sewanee Review, Stosvet, West Branch,
Bangor Daily News, Florida Review, Café Review, Pucker-
brush Review.*

"The Oil Man" was read on *All Things Considered* on Nation-
al Public Radio. "Hebrew School (1955)" appeared on Poetry
Daily. "The Novel of Alcohol" was reprinted in *The Breath of
Parted Lips: Voices from the Robert Frost Place, vol. 2.* "The
Torture Channel" was reprinted in *Cut Loose the Body: An
Anthology of Poems on Torture and Fernando Botero's Abu
Ghraib Paintings.*

CavanKerry's Mission

Through publishing and programming, CavanKerry Press connects communities of writers with communities of readers. We publish poetry that reaches from the page to include the reader, by the finest new and established contemporary writers. Our programming brings our books and our poets to people where they live, cultivating new audiences and nourishing established ones.

Other Books in the Notable Voices Series